W9-AUI-798

PROTECTING the EARTH'S ANIMALS

# Saving Ocean Animals

## Sharks, Turtles, Coral, and Fish

MICHAEL CENTORE

**Animal Testing:**
**Attacking a Controversial Problem**

**Battling Wildlife Poachers:**
**The Fight to Save Elephants, Rhinos, Lions, Tigers, and More**

**Dogs and Cats:**
**Saving Our Precious Pets**

**Pollination Problems:**
**The Battle to Save Bees and Other Vital Animals**

**Rescuing Primates:**
**Gorillas, Chimps, and Monkeys**

**Saving Marine Mammals:**
**Whales, Dolphins, Seals, and More**

**Saving Ocean Animals:**
**Sharks, Turtles, Coral, and Fish**

**Saving the Rainforests:**
**Inside the World's Most Diverse Habitat**

# Saving Ocean Animals

## Sharks, Turtles, Coral, and Fish

BY MICHAEL CENTORE

**Mason Crest**
450 Parkway Drive, Suite D
Broomall, PA 19008
www.masoncrest.com



Printed and bound in the United States of America.

Series ISBN: 978-1-4222-3872-1
Hardback ISBN: 978-1-4222-3879-0
EBook ISBN: 978-1-4222-7916-8

First printing
1 3 5 7 9 8 6 4 2

Produced by Shoreline Publishing Group LLC
Santa Barbara, California
Editorial Director: James Buckley Jr.
Designer: Patty Kelley
www.shorelinepublishing.com

Library of Congress Cataloging-in-Publication Data
Names: Centore, Michael, 1980- author.
Title: Saving ocean animals : sharks, turtles, coral, and fish / by Michael Centore.
Description: Broomall, PA : Mason Crest, [2017] |
Series: Protecting the Earth's animals | Includes bibliographical references and index.
Identifiers: LCCN 2017001352| ISBN 9781422238790 (hardback) | ISBN 9781422238721 (series) | ISBN 9781422279168 (ebook)
Subjects: LCSH: Marine animals–Conservation–Juvenile literature. | Wildlife conservation–Juvenile literature. | Marine ecology–Juvenile literature.
Classification: LCC QL122.2 .C45 2017 | DDC 333.95/16–dc23 LC record available at https://lccn.loc.gov/2017001352

Cover photographs by Dreamstime.com: Theo Gottwald (fish); foryourinfo (turtle).
Vision Dive/Shutterstock (shark)

## QR Codes disclaimer:

# CONTENTS



## KEY ICONS TO LOOK FOR

**Words to Understand:** These words with their easy-to-understand definitions will increase the reader's understanding of the text, while building vocabulary skills.

**Sidebars:** This boxed material within the main text allows readers to build knowledge, gain insights, explore possibilities, and broaden their perspectives by weaving together additional information to provide realistic and holistic perspectives.

**Educational Videos:** Readers can view videos by scanning our QR codes, providing them with additional educational content to supplement the text. Examples include news coverage, moments in history, speeches, iconic moments, and much more!

**Text-Dependent Questions:** These questions send the reader back to the text for more careful attention to the evidence presented here.

**Research Projects:** Readers are pointed toward areas of further inquiry connected to each chapter. Suggestions are provided for projects that encourage deeper research and analysis.

**Series Glossary of Key Terms:** This back-of-the-book glossary contains terminology used throughout this series. Words found here increase the reader's ability to read and comprehend higher-level books and articles in this field.

# INTRODUCTION

**In the middle of the North Pacific Ocean, between the east coast of Japan and the west coast of North America, lies the Great Pacific Garbage Patch.** While the name may bring to mind an image of a huge, floating continent of litter, it's actually a huge blob of tiny particles called *microplastics*. These are the remnants of plastic items (like water bottles, for instance) that have been broken down by the sun over time. However, even the sun can't break plastic down completely, and the microplastic particles cloud the sea like little granules of sand.

Mixed in with the microplastics is other debris, from over 700,000 tons of fishing nets to stray toys and computer parts.

Circular ocean currents draw this litter into the center of the Garbage Patch. One estimate has the core of the patch at 386,000 square miles (about a million square kilometers), with an outer layer extending over 1.3 million square miles (3.36 million sq km). In addition to this, 70 percent of plastic sinks to the ocean floor.

All of this has a tremendous effect on the health of aquatic ecosystems. Fish, sea turtles, and whales die from ingesting this contaminated water. Seals drown after swimming into plastic fishing nets; a sea turtle or an albatross may confuse plastic for food. Coral eat the microplastics, but get no nutrition from them and starve. Coral are important because they take in carbon dioxide and provide vital nutrients to marine life.

**Sea animal? No, a deadly plastic bag.**

The Garbage Patch affects ocean species in less direct ways, too: it blocks sunlight from getting to algae and plankton below. Such creatures are the first link in the ocean's food chain. If they lack the sun's energy, they can't produce the vital nutrients that feed other, bigger animals like turtles; the more of these animals that die, the less food there is for sharks and other predators. One way or another, the entire food chain suffers. Eventually, plastics ingested by fish can work their way up the food chain, and humans end up consuming them.

If the Garbage Patch represents how humans can drastically affect our ocean environment for the worse, it is also an opportunity to show how we can affect it for the better. One young Dutch inventor, Boyan Slat, has designed a system of floating barriers and screens to trap debris on the open ocean. A prototype for the system was launched on the North Sea in the Netherlands in June 2016.

In addition to massive threats like the Garbage Patch, ocean animals face other dangers, from overfishing to pollution to the rising temperatures and sea levels caused by climate change. Read on for profiles of how four groups of these animals—sharks, turtles, coral, and fish—are impacted by these threats, as well as how people are trying to help them. You may be inspired to pitch in, too—water is the basis of life, and our survival as a species depends on the health of our oceans.

## WORDS TO UNDERSTAND

**ampullae of Lorenzi** sensing organs found in sharks and rays that can detect electrical signals from other animals

**benthic** of or relating to the bottom of a body of water

**cartilage** a firm, flexible tissue, found in the skeletons of young vertebrates and other animals

**embryo** an unborn animal that is still in the process of development

**pelagic** of or relating to the waters of open oceans or seas

# SHARKS

**No doubt about it—sharks are pretty ferocious-looking animals.** With their sharp teeth and agile swimming ability, they are one of the top predators in the ocean's ecosystem. This means that they eat many creatures, but few creatures can eat them. Since they don't have to worry too much about being attacked, they can move freely through different aquatic habitats, from deep oceans to shallow coastal regions. Some shark species can even live in freshwater bodies of water like rivers and lakes. **Pelagic** sharks stick to the open ocean and seas, while **benthic** sharks dwell at the bottom of the ocean.

## Shark Traits

There are more than 400 species of sharks. Some are more well known than others, such as the great white shark and the hammerhead shark. But some of the lesser-known species are fascinating, too: consider the dwarf lanternshark, which, at a mere 8 inches (20 cm), could fit in a human hand. The largest is the whale shark, which has been recorded at a length of 40 feet (12.2 m).

No matter their size, all sharks have certain things in common. Their skeletons are made of **cartilage**, the same type of tough, rubbery connective tissue that makes up the human ears and nose. Sharks have multiple rows of teeth; the average is 15 rows, though the bull shark can have as many as fifty. The front rows of teeth are what the shark uses to tear into prey. As teeth fall out, new teeth from the rear rows slide up to take their place. Some sharks may go through thirty thousand teeth in a lifetime. All sharks breathe through gills, which are slits on the sides of their bodies. There may be five to seven of these slits, which take oxygen in from the water and filter it through tiny blood vessels into the blood. The heart pumps carbon dioxide back out through the gills and into the water.

Sharks have the same five senses that humans do:

**The slits on the shark's side let in oxygen-giving seawater.**

sight, hearing, touch, taste, and smell. Their sense of scent is especially acute so they can hunt prey in the deep, dark oceans. Sharks have nostrils on the underside of their snout that are used only for smelling. This allows them to detect tiny amounts of chemicals in vast stretches of water. The lemon shark, for instance, can pick up the scent of tuna from just a few drops of its oil, and the great white can sniff out prey from up to three miles (4.8 km) away.

In addition to the five major senses, sharks have small pores near their nostrils called **ampullae of Lorenzi** that can detect electrical signals generated by the muscle movements of other animals. They use this process to locate

## TYPES OF TEETH

Depending on their diet, sharks have one of four different kinds of teeth. Those that dwell on the bottom of the ocean and have to crack open shellfish for food have hard, flat teeth. Long, pointy teeth are good for sharks who need to snag slippery fish. Great whites and other sharks that feed on large mammals like seals, sea lions, and dolphins have a combination of pointed lower teeth and triangular upper teeth to tear flesh into small pieces. Finally, sharks that feed on plankton—microscopic organisms that drift through the ocean—and tiny crustaceans called krill have tiny, nonfunctional teeth (left). These sharks simply take water in through their mouths and filter out the food.

prey as well as navigate through the water. A "seventh sense" known as the lateral line allows sharks to feel subtle changes in the pressure and direction of water currents. Pores similar to the ampullae of Lorenzi line the length of both sides of the shark's body. The pores open into canals beneath the skin with cells that sense movement. Sharks use the lateral line to detect information about their surroundings.

## History and Evolution

One thing's for sure: the shark is a survivor. As a species, sharks have been around for some 450 million years. They've survived all five major mass extinction events, adapted to different aquatic environments, and changed their shapes and features to stay on top of the food chain.

All sharks descend from a group of bony fish called acanthodians. These "spiny sharks" appeared around 440 million years ago and lived for 160 million years before going extinct. In addition to looking like sharks, they began to acquire the shark's trademark cartilage skeleton. The first modern-looking shark, *Cladoselache*, followed about 370 million years ago. *Cladoselache* grew up to 6 feet (2 m) long and had a forked tail and pointed teeth. Beginning around 360 million years ago, sharks really began to diversify, taking on unique characteristics like the anvil-shaped fin of *Stethacanthus*. In fact, there was such an explosion of shark species during this period that it's come to be known as the "Golden Age" of sharks.

Around 252 million years ago, a mass extinction wiped out 90 percent of ocean life. Scientists believe that sharks survived by swimming deeper in the seas. Many of the traits we associate with sharks today began to appear in time that followed, known as the Jurassic Period, about 200 million years ago. These included flexible jaws for swallowing large prey and tails that could help them swim faster across greater distances. In all, 12 new families of shark appeared during the Jurassic Period.

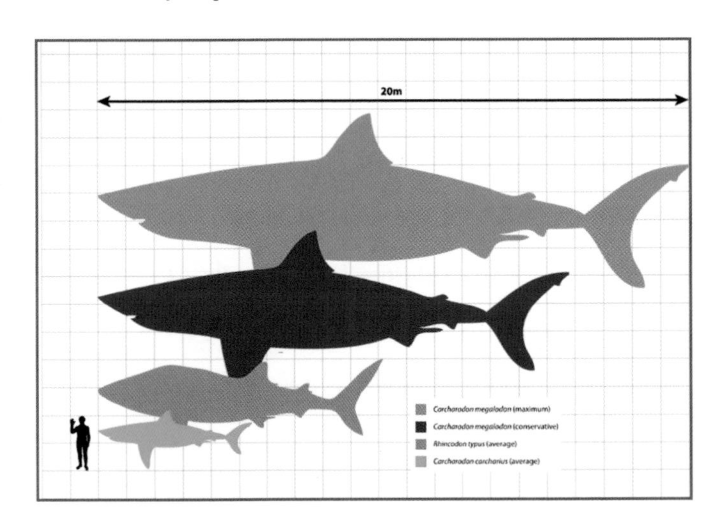


**The grey and red sharks are prehistoric; purple is a whale shark.**

Several of the sharks still alive today had their origins in the Cretaceous Period, about 145 to 65 million years ago. During this time,

## SHARK FOSSILS

We know about the history of sharks by studying fossils. Fossils are the preserved remains of once-living beings. Hard parts of a creature's body, such as bones or shells, fossilize better than soft parts because the soft parts decay more easily. The shark's cartilage skeleton doesn't fossilize well, but its teeth do. Some shark teeth fossilize when they fall to the ocean floor and are covered with sediment. This protects them from decay. Over thousands of years, minerals from the water leech through the sediment and into the pores of the teeth. The minerals plus the pressure of the sediment cause the teeth to harden into fossils. The oldest shark teeth to have been discovered are 400 million years old.

Sometimes shark scales are fossilized, too. Preserved scales found in Colorado date back 455 million years, though scientists debate whether they are actually from a shark-like species. Scales found in Siberia and Mongolia that date back 420 million years are more commonly accepted as the earliest evidence of sharks.

SharkSavers in action

sharks evolved to become top predators of the sea, and even acquired unique features like the ability to glow in the dark to communicate in low-light conditions. Another mass extinction occurred at the end of the Cretaceous Period, and once again many species survived. These survivors developed into the sharks we know today. One example is the hammerhead shark, which began to evolve "only" 20 million years ago.

## Saving Sharks

Scientists are still finding new species of shark, like the ninja lanternshark, originally located in 2010 off the Pacific Coast of Central America and identified in 2015. The ninja lanternshark has jet-black skin and can glow in the dark. But even with such exciting discoveries, the shark population is under severe threat. An estimated 100 million sharks are killed every year due to human activities, such as harvesting fins for shark-fin soup, a delicacy in some countries. The process of "finning," as it is commonly known, is particularly gruesome: poachers cut the fins off of sharks, then toss the sharks back into the ocean, often while the animals are still alive. Because they can't swim

**Aiming for smaller fish, these nets brought up sharks, too.**

without their fins, the sharks are left to sink to the seafloor, where they either die of suffocation or blood loss or are devoured by other animals. This makes sharks some of the most endangered animals on the planet.

Fortunately, there are several organizations worldwide dedicated to preserving sharks. The American group Shark-Savers, a part of the WildAid organization that fights the illegal sale of wild animals and products, works to end the shark-fin trade. They use education, the idea of establishing "shark sanctuaries" in various countries, and divers to record data about shark populations.

The Shark Trust fights similar battles from the United Kingdom, partnering with conservation organizations around

**Inside the see-through egg case is a small sharky embryo.**

the world that advocate for sharks. One of their projects, the Great Eggcase Hunt, trains beachcombers of all ages to identify and catalog empty eggcases they find on UK shores. (Eggcases are the tough pouches that contain shark **embryos**; after the sharks hatch, the eggcases often wash up onto the sand.) Gathering information on eggcases helps scientists determine where young sharks are nursing and how species are distributed—both of which help focus conservation efforts.

Not all shark activism is being spearheaded by organizations—individuals have gotten into the mix, too. In his 2006 documentary film, *Sharkwater*, writer and director Rob Stewart explores places where shark hunting is especially active, including Costa Rica and Ecuador. The film shows how shark hunting is contributing to shark extinction and highlights the many ways sharks help the ecosystem.

Another shark activist with ties to the film world was Peter Benchley. Benchley was the author of *Jaws*, a 1974 book about a great white shark that terrorizes a small town. It was later turned into a movie by director Steven Spielberg. During a deep-sea dive off Costa Rica in the early 1980s, Benchley witnessed something that would change his life forever: the ocean floor was littered with the corpses of finned sharks. This horrifying image made Benchley realize that humans are more of a threat to sharks than sharks are to humans. He regretted his negative portrayal of the great white in *Jaws*, and spent much of the remainder of his career campaigning for shark conservation.

## TEXT-DEPENDENT QUESTIONS

1. What are sharks' skeletons made of?
2. What are some examples of traits sharks developed during the Jurassic Period?
3. What is shark "finning" and why is it dangerous?

## RESEARCH PROJECT

Research a few different types of prehistoric sharks, such as *Elegestolepis*, *Edestus*, and *Hybodus*. And check out *Megaladon*! Write a brief report about their traits, habits, body structure, and other notable characteristics. Include any possible reasons for why they went extinct.

## WORDS TO UNDERSTAND

**herbaceous** describing an animal that eats plants

**incubate** referring to the temperature and conditions of eggs before they hatch

**keratin** a protein that makes up the structure of hair, claws, hooves, horns, and other animal parts

**metabolism** the physical, chemical, and biological processes that sustain the life of an organism

**nomenclature** a system for naming things

**omnivore** an animal that eats both plants and animals

**poaching** illegally capturing wild animals

# TURTLES

**One of the oldest members of the reptile class, the humble turtle is widely known for several of its characteristics.** Its hard, often geometrically patterned shell; its reputation for moving slowly (though not as slowly as you might think); and its habit of ducking its head inside its shell to hide from predators. There are over 300 turtle species living in almost every one of the world's climates, and some of them can get quite large—consider the leatherback sea turtle, which, weighing over a thousand pounds (453 kg), is the fourth biggest reptile on earth. Turtles are also remarkably long-lived creatures. Even standard pet turtles can live to be 80 years old (provided there is someone around long enough to take care of them), and larger species more than 100 years. A popular theory as to why turtles can live so long is their slow **metabolism**: since they use energy at a slower rate, they are able to conserve more for the long haul.

## Shell Games

The first step in learning about turtles is to get the **nomenclature** right: while people often use the terms *turtle*, *terrapin*, and *tortoise* interchangeably, they're actually each different types of animals. All three are members of the animal order Testudines. Technically, turtles live mostly in water—freshwater (like ponds and lakes) and in the ocean's saltwater. They have webbed feet or flippers to help them swim, and they are **omnivores**, meaning they eat both plants and animals. Tortoises live on land. They have large feet that are much better for walking than swimming. They tend to eat only plants. Finally, terrapins are a kind of combination of turtles and tortoises: they live both on land and in water, usually in swampy areas.

Even with these definitions, most people use the term *turtle* to describe any member of the Testudines order. Testudines are characterized by their hard, bony shells, and a powerful flat beak, or mouth, made of **keratin** instead of teeth. There are two main parts of a turtle's shell: the upper part that covers the back of the body is called the carapace, while the lower part that protects the belly is called the plastron. A turtle's shell is made of fused bones of the ribs and spine. This means that the shell is really part of the turtle's skeleton, so it can't detach from the shell or leave it behind. The shell is covered with keratin plates called *scutes* for extra protection. Instead of scutes, softshell turtles have a layer of tough, leathery skin over their bony shells.

**Sea turtles shells have overlapping "scutes."**

Turtles can be classified by how they tuck their heads into their shells. They do this one of two ways: *hidden-necked* turtles can draw their head and neck straight back into their shells; *side-necked* turtles must tuck their head and neck in sideways under the edge of the shell near the shoulder. Side-necked turtles are only found in the Southern Hemisphere. Many species of both types can pull their legs and tail into their shells as well. Some, like mud turtles, are even able to enclose their upper and lower shells around their bodies once their heads, legs, and tails are inside. In addition to protecting them from predators, this wards off the beating sun on hot days so they don't overheat or get too dry. On the other hand, sea turtles cannot go into their shells at all: the flippers they have instead of legs to help them swim are too large, and their heads are always exposed too.

Turtles have other defenses besides their shells. Mud and musk turtles can release a pungent fluid called musk. Its odor is powerful enough to repel predators. Snapping

**Leatherback sea turtles struggle to move on land.**

turtles have long necks and powerful jaws, and they can reach out and bite at anything—or anyone—who comes close enough to frighten them. Its spiny tail and sharp claws that can scratch are other ways it defends itself. These defenses are very important because the snapping turtle can't pull its legs, arms, or head into its shell, leaving it vulnerable to attack.

Sea turtle babies break out!

## Sea Turtles

There are approximately 300 known species of turtle, and nearly half face the threat of extinction. This is a very alarming statistic considering that turtles have been living on earth for 220 million years, outlasting the dinosaurs. Among the most threatened turtles are the seven species of sea turtle: green, leatherback, Kemp's ridley, loggerhead, hawksbill, olive ridley, and flatback. Of these, five are classified by the International Union for Conservation of Nature (IUCN) as "endangered," meaning that they face a high risk of extinction in the near future. One, the leatherback, is classified as "vulnerable." Its population has been steadily declining over the past several years and is predicted to continue. There is still not enough data for the IUCN to classify the flatback sea turtle, partially because it's only found in certain waters around Australia, Papua New Guinea, and Indonesia. However, they are listed as vulnerable by the Australian government.

The main difference between sea turtles and other species is that sea turtles have flipper-like fins instead of legs. Their front flippers power them through the water, while the rear ones act as rudders, steering them as they swim. Sea turtles have more streamlined bodies than land-based turtles to help them maneuver swiftly. Some sea turtles are **herbaceous**, meaning they eat plants such as algae and seaweed. Others eat meat, including shrimp, jellyfish, and mollusks. Females may migrate more than a thousand miles (c. 1,600 km) from their feeding grounds to the nesting sites where they were born to lay their eggs. The mother comes ashore, digs a hole in the sand with her rear flippers, and lays a group of fifty to more than a hundred eggs called a clutch. She then buries the clutch and returns to the water. The young hatchlings that emerge from the eggs are left to fend for themselves.

The main threats to sea turtles are from humans: **poaching** for meat, eggs, and shells; destruction of their

**The tragic meeting of sea turtle and fishing nets ends badly.**

natural habitats through water pollution, overdevelopment, and climate change; and getting caught in marine debris such as plastic fishing nets. They also face natural threats, including birds, raccoons, and other predators who eat hatchlings, the young turtles that have just emerged from their eggs.

Global warming could have a drastic impact on sea turtle populations. Rising sea levels would mean less beach area and therefore fewer places for mother turtles to lay their eggs. Increased temperatures could even impact the gender of sea turtles. Turtle eggs that **incubate** above 85 degrees Fahrenheit tend to be female. Warmer sands would mean warmer nesting sites, and therefore more females than males. If this trend continued, it would mean fewer opportunities for sea turtles to reproduce new offspring.

## TURTLE TEARS

If you are ever fortunate enough to watch the spectacle of a sea turtle coming ashore to lay her eggs, she might seem to be doing something unexpected: crying. One legend has it that these mother turtles are weeping for their children (fitting, since only one in a thousand sea turtle hatchlings will survive into adulthood). But the truth is, these tears are just the turtle getting rid of excess salt from the seawater it drinks.

## Protecting and Conserving

The world has been aware of the plight of sea turtles for quite some time. In the United States, the Endangered Species Act has declared five species of sea turtles as either endangered or threatened since the 1970s. This means that it is illegal to harm sea turtles, their hatchlings, or their eggs in any way, or to import (bring something into the country) or sell sea turtles or any sea turtle products. Individual states where there are large populations of sea turtles have their own regulations, too. In Florida, for instance, the Marine Turtle Protection Act allows state authorities to protect sea turtles in the best ways they see fit. In 1981, an international agreement made it illegal to trade sea turtles, including their eggs, shells, and meat.

It's not only governmental organizations that are doing the hard work of protecting sea turtles. Individuals like Dr. Mariana Fuentes, a Brazilian marine biologist now living in Australia, are on the front lines of analyzing sea turtle behavior. They monitor nesting sites, observe how climate change impacts sea turtle habitats, and perform other data collection and lab work to manage sea turtle populations.

A visit to a manta ray feeding area in the Cayman Islands spurred Dr. Fuentes's interest in marine biology.

**Dr. Maria Fuentes and her friend at a Barbados dive site.**

Fascinated by the rays' behavior, she began asking other marine biologists about them. She went on to study marine biology and environmental science at James Cook University in Townsville, Australia, eventually obtaining her PhD with a project about climate change and green sea turtles in the Great Barrier Reef. As of 2015 she is an assistant professor at Florida State University. She has worked on sea turtle projects with governments and other organizations in places as diverse as Madagascar and Barbados.

In an interview with *National Geographic*, Dr. Fuentes cited sea turtles' "beauty, persistence, [and] strength" as her inspiration for wanting to work with and conserve them. In another interview with the Scientista Foundation, an organization dedicated to educating young women about careers in science, technology, engineering, and math, she gave some advice to aspiring marine biologists: learn about all the different avenues of marine biology to see which one appeals to you. If possible, try to volunteer with a marine biology or conservation organization to get some practical knowledge as well.

## TEXT-DEPENDENT QUESTIONS

1. What is the difference between a turtle, a terrapin, and a tortoise?
2. Do turtles have other defenses besides their shells? If so, name one.
3. What are the main threats to the lives of sea turtles?

## RESEARCH PROJECT

Select one of the seven species of sea turtle mentioned in this chapter. Research its history, characteristics, traits, habitats, and other important information. Write a brief report summarizing what you've found. Be sure to include any organizations, individuals, or governmental agencies trying to conserve the species, and how they are going about it.

## WORDS TO UNDERSTAND

**coral bleaching** when corals eject the algae that live in them due to high water temperatures

**greenhouse gas** a gas in the atmosphere, such as carbon dioxide, that absorbs heat and increases the earth's temperature

**lagoon** a shallow body of water separated from a larger body by a sandbank or reef

**photosynthesis** the process where plants use sunlight, water, and carbon dioxide to create food and release oxygen

**polyp** in this case, a small sea animal with a tube-shaped body

**salinity** the amount of salt in a solution

**secrete** to discharge something, such as a fluid

**symbiotic** referring to organisms that live together, usually to help each other

# CORAL

**At first glance, coral seems a strange thing to try and classify.** Its hard, textured appearance makes it look like a rock. Its spiny, almost leaf-like tentacles (plus the way it "roots" to the seafloor) give it the appearance of a plant. The truth is, coral is neither of these. Coral are living things, unlike rocks, and because they do not make their own food they are not plants. It's hard to imagine since we can't see their faces, mouths, or other body parts, but coral are actually animals related to jellyfish.

## Basic Structure

The underwater structures we refer to as coral are really thousands of tiny living

**The tiny arms of coral reach out to seek food in the water.**

creatures called polyps. Polyps have a cylindrical or tube-like shape and are usually only a few millimeters in diameter, though some can be larger. Think of them like cans open at the top: around the "mouth" are tentacles with stinging cells that capture small fish and plankton, which the coral can digest as food. Inside the polyps are cells of an algae called zooxanthellae. The algae and the coral polyps have a symbiotic relationship: the polyps make carbon dioxide and water, which the algae use to turn sunlight into energy in the process of photosynthesis. The algae then "feed" this energy of sugars, fats, and oxygen back to the coral. This cycle continues and sustains the lives of both.

Coral polyps called hard or stony corals take calcium carbonate, also known as limestone, from the sea and use it to create a cup-shaped skeleton. These skeletons attach to rock or the structures of dead skeletons. The polyp rests in the skeleton to protect its body. As polyps reproduce over time, they continue to **secrete** calcium carbonate and build up the distinctive shapes of corals. Not all coral polyps create skeletons, however; those known as soft corals have spines in their bodies to give them support.

## Reproduction

Corals have a variety of reproductive methods. They can be male, female, or hermaphroditic, meaning they are both male and female. They can also produce either asexually (by themselves) or sexually. There are four major ways corals reproduce asexually:

- **Budding:** Here, a new polyp "buds" off an older one, forming a growth. After this new polyp reaches maturity, it breaks away from the original polyp and settles elsewhere.
- **Bailout:** Sometimes a polyp will just leave its colony (a group of many identical polyps sharing a common skeleton), find another place to attach itself, and start creating a new colony.

- **Fragmentation:** When a large part of a coral colony breaks apart, it can form a new colony. This tends to happen when colonies are subject to a sudden shock, such as getting damaged during a storm.
- **Fission:** This occurs when polyps divide themselves. After division, the edges of the polyps close, creating two separate, whole polyps.

Corals reproduce sexually by broadcasting, also known as broadcast spawning. This means that corals release sperm and eggs into the water, where they join together to create larvae. The larvae will eventually develop into polyps. Broadcast spawning usually happens just once a year. It is an incredible thing to watch. Because male and female corals cannot physically reproduce with one another, they must time the release of sperm and eggs perfectly so they can meet and fertilize in the water. Certain environmental factors influence the timing of broadcast spawning, including temperature, day length, tide level, and even the cycles of the moon.

In contrast to broadcast spawning, brooding corals release only sperm into the water. It floats down to eggs waiting inside the polyps, where fertilization occurs. After fertilization, the polyps release larvae. These "brooders" reproduce more frequently than broadcasting corals.

## Colonies and Reefs

Coral colonies can become very large, but the process is a slow one. Most corals grow an average of less than an inch a year, though some can grow as many as six inches. Different factors impact growth rates, from the **salinity** of the ocean water to temperature to available sunlight. As they grow, corals take on distinctive shapes called growth forms. Some main types of growth forms include: branching corals, which resemble antlers or tree branches as they fork out; digitate corals, with thin, finger-like projections; columnar corals, which are similar to digitate but form thicker pillars; encrusting corals that keep low and spread over a surface; and massive corals that grow into boulder-like structures that can be as large as a house.

**Coral forms will take root on just about anything, such as shell.**

When lots of coral colonies grow near each other, a coral reef is formed. Coral reefs are massive ecosystems that support the life of many different species. In fact, they're sometimes called the "rainforests of the sea" for their biological diversity. The Great Barrier Reef off the eastern coast of Australia is around 20,000 years old and the largest living thing on earth, and most other reefs are between 5,000 and 10,000 years old.

To put their importance into perspective, consider that coral reefs only take up 1 percent of the ocean floor, but support 25 percent of all ocean creatures. Fish, shrimp, crabs, and mollusks are just a few examples of animals that live in reefs. Some use the coral and their algae as food. Reefs even help support life outside of the ocean, such as

**An overhead view of a tiny part of the Great Barrier Reef.**

protecting the roots of mangrove trees and seagrasses that grow near the water from erosion. In turn, the mangroves and grasses provide food and breeding grounds for many reef animals, and protect the reefs from pollutants.

Reefs take shape in one of three major ways. Fringing reefs attach to a shore and spread outward into the sea. Barrier reefs build up near shorelines, but are separated by water channels or deep **lagoons**. Finally, atoll reefs are circular or arc shaped. They form around the rims of old oceanic volcanoes. As the volcanoes sink beneath sea level and the corals grow upward, ring-shaped reefs are created, enclosing open lagoons.

## Coral Bleaching

Despite the hardiness and durability of coral, they are struggling due to changes in the environment of the oceans. Rising temperatures, increased acidity in oceans due to greater carbon dioxide levels in the atmosphere, and water pollution all threaten the health of coral reefs worldwide. Warmer water temperatures can contribute to **coral bleaching**, which is when corals become stressed and release the zooxanthellae algae that live in them. Since this algae is responsible for a coral's color, the coral turns pale white, looking bleached. Bleached corals are still alive, but they have a harder time staying nourished. If a coral remains bleached for a long time, it can die.

**Time lapse of coral bleaching.**

For many years, coral bleaching was a pretty rare phenomenon. This began to change in 1979. Between that year and 1990, sixty instances of coral bleaching were reported from places all over the world. In 1998, an underwater heat wave caused by the weather system El Niño killed off 16 percent of the world's coral reefs. A similar effect occurred again in 2010, as record-high ocean temperatures ravaged reefs in Indonesia, Malaysia, and elsewhere. In 2015, the National Oceanic and Atmospheric Administration (NOAA) presented evidence of a third major mass bleaching event that began in the summer of 2014 and is projected to continue into 2017. This would make it the longest mass coral bleaching in history. It has already threatened 40 percent of the world's coral reefs.

Damage to reefs works its way up the food chain. Small fish can no longer use coral for food and shelter, the larger fish who eat them lose their main food source, and the birds who depend on the larger fish are affected, too. The good news is that some bleached reefs can recover under the proper conditions, though it may take ten years or more. For reefs to recover, they can't be exposed to high water temperatures for too long, there can't be pollutants in the water, and they must be free of other stresses like overfishing.

## DOCUMENTING THE DAMAGE

Since about half a billion people live within 60 miles of a reef and depend on it for food, protection against erosion, and jobs and income, many scientists say it's important to secure the long-term health of our reefs. One man, Richard Vevers, felt the task so crucial that he left his job as an advertising executive to start Ocean Agency, a nonprofit organization dedicated to helping marine environments. One of his main projects is documenting the world's reefs with underwater cameras. In 2016, he took extensive photos of the northern section of the Great Barrier Reef, showing damage throughout.

Even if they do recover, bleached reefs are not as healthy. They are more susceptible to microbes in the water that can lead to infection, and their ability to reproduce is weakened.

Because 93 percent of excess heat generated by humans is absorbed by the oceans, the surest way to guard against coral bleaching is to reduce greenhouse gas emissions that warm the surface of the planet. Many ways to save coral reefs are in our hands. Cutting back on fossil fuels by driving less or using public transport, conserving water, and reducing the use of fertilizers that make their way into our oceans (and can cause seaweed to build up

**The Vevers/NOAA study made this composite image.**

and smother corals) are a few starter solutions. On a larger level, governments have established more marine protected areas—places where human activities are closely monitored—to protect reefs.

## Reef 2050 in Australia

The effort to help save coral reefs is underway in places around the globe. With its monumental Great Barrier Reef system, Australia has many reef-related charities and scientific organizations working to protect and manage these fragile ocean ecosystems for years to come. These include the Great Barrier Reef Foundation, the Australian Marine Conservation Society, and the Great Barrier Reef Marine Park Authority, administered by the Australian government.

In March 2015, the Australian government released its Reef 2050 Plan, a long-term sustainability plan designed to ensure the reef's protection through 2050. Some of its major goals involve cutting down on the amount of dredged material (sediments and other waste gathered from the ocean floor) disposed of near the reef, putting in place lower-impact farming practices that improve water quality, and regulating fishing to protect marine animals.

Despite its many concrete proposals and a projected investment of $2 billion (Australian) over the next decade, the Reef 2050 Plan has been met with criticism since its inception. Some environmental experts have said it does not do enough to address the root causes of coral bleaching and reef destruction. They point to the fact that the plan does not address climate change directly or provide means of reducing greenhouse gas emissions in Australia that impact the reef. They also question the decision to continue hazardous practices such as coal mining while trying to save the reef.

Sadly, the critics appear to have been correct. In November 2016, news broke that the Great Barrier Reef experienced some of the worst damage in its history after the Reef 2050 Plan began. In a brief nine-month span through 2016, 67 percent of the reef in the once-pristine northern section suffered severe bleaching due to warming water. The coral is expected to grow back within 15 years, but only if water temperatures do not continue to increase.

**The survival of the reefs is crucial to many fish.**

In the midst of such devastation, there is room for hope: this, the third major bleaching event in the reef since 1998, seems to have served as a wakeup call for the Australian authorities in charge of the Reef 2050 Plan. They recognize the need to accelerate the actions outlined on the plan, starting with enforcing rules against pesticides and fertilizers in farms across the country. There is also $2.55 billion (Australian) set aside for an fund that will aim to reduce Australia's emissions to 5 percent below 2000 levels by 2020.

## TEXT-DEPENDENT QUESTIONS

1. How do algae and coral polyps help each other?
2. Name and describe two types of coral growth forms.
3. What is coral bleaching and how is it caused?

## RESEARCH PROJECT

Research one of the world's major coral reefs, such as the Great Barrier Reef, the Red Sea Coral Reef, or the Florida Reef. Find out about its geological history and how it came to be formed, the marine life it supports, and the threats it faces and any ways it is being protected. Write a brief report summarizing your findings.

## WORDS TO UNDERSTAND

**anadromous** describing a fish that lives in both fresh- and saltwater

**buoyancy** the upward force that allows objects to float

**cartilaginous** made of or relating to cartilage

**fishery** an area where fish are caught for commercial purposes

**migratory** of or relating to migration, the movement of animals

**symmetrical** when two halves of something, such as a body, look the same

**tetrapods** four-limbed animals that live on land, including amphibians, birds, reptiles, mammals, and some extinct species such as dinosaurs

**vertebrate** an animal with a backbone

# FISH

**Like reptiles, fish are one of the five major classes of vertebrates, animals that have a backbone.** They live in the water and breathe through slits called gills. (For more info on how gills work, see chapter 1.) Fish are cold blooded, meaning their body temperature changes depending on their surroundings—if they're in chilly water, their internal temperature will be cold, but if they move to warmer water or into the sunlight it will rise. It's estimated that there are over 30,000 species of fish in the world today, about half of which live in the oceans.

## Fish Evolution

The first creatures that resembled fish appeared some 530 million years ago. They didn't look entirely like fish, but they had some traits that fish would later adapt, like a separate head and tail, a **symmetrical** body, and a nerve cord that ran the length of their body. Because these creatures had no jaws, they ate by straining food particles out

### FISH TO THE LAND!

Even though there are only a few species of lobe-finned fish alive today, including the lungfish and the very rare coelacanth, they left a lasting impact on the evolutionary chain. Their strong fins evolved into limbs, allowing them to climb out of the water and walk on land. This means that lobe-finned fish are the ancestors of all **tetrapods** (four-limbed animals that live on land)—and that includes us! There are an estimated 28,000 species of bony fish, making them the largest class of vertebrates alive today.

of the water, a process called filter feeding.

Jawless fish were the dominant species of the next wave of fish evolution, which began around 490 million years ago. Besides lacking a lower jaw, these fish had bony plates on their heads to protect against other predators of the sea. Later versions of these fish developed tails to help them move more swiftly through the water. The first fish with jaws appeared over 416 million years ago, during the Silurian Period.

It was the following period, the Devonian, when fish species really began to diversify—so much so that this period is sometimes referred to as the "Age of Fishes." Jawed fishes called placoderms prowled through freshwater and ocean habitats with sharp, powerful plates that functioned as teeth. Placoderms went extinct by the end of the Devonian Period, around 360 million years ago.

One reason for placoderm extinction was the rise of two other types of jawed fish: those with **cartilaginous** skeletons and those with bony skeletons. Cartilaginous fish had scales and sharp teeth; they later developed into sharks and rays. Bony fish had scales, fins, and a special gas-filled "swim bladder" that they could use to control their **buoyancy**. They branched off into two distinct types: ray-finned fish and lobe-finned fish. Ray-finned fish have fins of fan-like, bony spines, while lobe-finned fish have fleshy fins that join to their bodies with a single bone.

## Freshwater and Saltwater Threats

One major difference between fish is whether they live in fresh water or salt water. Though only 2.5 percent of the world's water is fresh (and only 1 percent of that is easily accessible, not frozen into icecaps or snowfields), 40 percent of the world's fish live in freshwater environments. Some fish, called **anadromous** fish, live in both fresh and salt water. An example is the salmon, which travels up rivers from the ocean to deposit its eggs.

Both freshwater and saltwater fish face many environmental threats. Dams built on rivers can disrupt the migratory patterns of freshwater fish, and chemicals that drain into the water supply from farms and cities can cause harmful pollution. One of the gravest dangers to saltwater fish—and the ocean ecosystem as a whole—is overfishing. This is when more fish are taken out of the ocean than can be replaced by existing stock. The problem of overfishing stems from the fact that humans worldwide depend on fish for food. According to a study by the United Nations, fish made up

## AQUACULTURE

Aquaculture is the practice of raising fish in water environments, almost like you'd raise a cow or chicken for food. It's often referred to as "fish farming." Fish farming can be a good alternative to intensive trawling and other industrial fishing practices that can harm oceans: the fish are bred, raised, and harvested in more controlled environments, such as ponds, tanks, or cages. Though this can be a sustainable way of meeting world fish demand, it also has its drawbacks. Fish farms produce toxic animal waste and antibiotics (used to treat infections fish develop from living in cramped conditions) that wash into oceans. Farmed fish eat a lot of wild-caught fish like anchovies, which are already overfished throughout the world. Finally, animal rights activists argue that fish raised in fish farms are often stuffed into overcrowded conditions, where they lose their sense of direction and damage their fins.

17 percent of the world's animal protein intake in 2013; in some places, fish accounts for 25 percent of animal protein intake.

UN report on aquaculture

Overfishing is not a recent problem. In the 1800s, humans destroyed much of the world's whale population by overfishing for whale oil. In the mid-20th century, new programs to make high-protein foods cheaper and more widely available led to the rise of the industrial fishing industry. Between 1950 and 1994, fishing catches worldwide grew by 400 percent. This gave people access to a variety of fish at inexpensive prices, but the amount of available fish peaked around 1989. Since then, catches have steadily declined.

Today, the global fishing industry is two to three times larger than what the oceans can support. Industrial fishing methods such as bottom trawling—in which a large net is dragged across the ocean floor—damage ocean habitats by scooping up everything in their path. Sea turtles, dolphins, seabirds, corals, and all sorts of other marine animals are collected indiscriminately and hauled out of the ocean. Because they are not wanted (known as "by-catch"), they are often thrown back overboard, sometimes when they are dead or dying. A related problem is when nets get lost at sea. They are hard to recover and can end up trapping and killing wildlife long after the fishing boats have gone.

## Solutions to Overfishing

Overfishing is a serious problem—a 2010 study by the State of World Fisheries and Aquaculture showed that more than 50 percent of the world's fisheries are overfished. Tropical waters in places like West Africa are suffering too, as the global fishing industry expands into them. But there are signs of hope. One is a newfound awareness that the ocean, once thought to be a bottomless source of food, is

**Fish face a great threat from humankind's love of eating them.**

actually a living system that needs to be carefully tended. Governments, fishing organizations, and individuals have all proposed solutions to overfishing and the environmental hazards it creates.

Some of these solutions are actually pretty simple, like modifications to fishing equipment. Commercial longline fisheries, which use baited hooks that dangle off of a single fishing line several miles long, can tie streamers to their lines to warn seabirds of their presence. This way the birds don't get trapped in the lines as they try to take the bait. Fisheries can also use weighted lines that sink faster, or set lines out at nighttime when there are fewer birds. These methods have reduced fishing-related seabird deaths by more than 90 percent in some parts of the world.

**Fishing can be a fine hobby, but in small doses.**

Another solution is to place more of the ocean under protection. Less than 1 percent is currently protected, though that number is expected to increase within the next few years. Protected areas do not necessarily ban all fishing, but they do impose certain limitations. They also monitor building and development on shorelines and other threats to marine life. Some conservationists recommend even more radical approaches to protected areas, such as managing entire regions of the ocean as separate zones. This would set up different zones for different uses. Areas of the ocean that needed more protection, such as fish breeding grounds, would be off limits to certain activities.

New laws governing catch limits could also help protect against overfishing. One program that has had success is called catch sharing. Here, individual fishermen or fishing communities are given a secure amount of fish from a managed fishery. Because they know they have a guaranteed portion of the total catch, fishermen no longer need to compete with each other to grab the most fish. They can fish when they want and work together to ensure the fish population stays healthy. The more the population grows, the more fish they have to catch and sell. It not only brings economic rewards, but environmental ones too.

We are living in a time when human impact on the planet is at all-time high. Population growth, industrial practices, and large-scale farming operations, to name just a few issues, have altered the way we use the earth's resources. The interconnected nature of our planet means that change in one area has a direct effect on another. Rising air temperatures affect ocean temperatures, sea levels, and weather patterns worldwide. More carbon dioxide in the atmosphere leads more acidic oceans, which makes it harder for mollusks and other shellfish to build their shells. This may seem like a minor problem, but since so many species—including humans—rely on these animals for food, even a small disruption in the food web can impact our lives.

There is no sense in sugarcoating the issue: the health of our oceans, their animals, and our shoreline ecosystems

**The glorious return of salmon to their home pools to spawn.**

are facing serious threats. Fortunately, there are ways to help: small adjustments to our lifestyles like using fewer plastic products, reducing energy use, and joining up with an organization committed to protecting the oceans are some good places to start working for change. While we may not be conscious of them on a day-to-day basis, the security of our oceans is bound up in our survival as a species.

## TEXT-DEPENDENT QUESTIONS

1. What is filter feeding?

2. What is the difference between ray-finned fish and lobe-finned fish?

3. Name and describe two potential solutions for overfishing.

## RESEARCH PROJECT

Research a species of fish that is listed as endangered. Examples include the largetooth sawfish, the Atlantic sturgeon, and the Rio Grande silvery minnow. Write a brief report covering the evolutionary history of the fish, its natural habitat, the parts of the world where it is found, and any programs in place to help save it.

# HOW YOU CAN HELP

Inspired to pitch in and help change our oceans for the better? Check out some of these resources for ways you can get involved.

## Online Resources

The World Wildlife Fund is a great place to find information on land- and marine-based animals that may be in danger. A special "How to Help" section highlights ways you can assist in the global conservation effort. (www.worldwildlife.org)

The website of the National Oceanic and Atmospheric Administration (NOAA) is a great place to educate yourself about fisheries, marine sanctuaries, and other topics related to the life of the ocean. (www.noaa.gov)

## Organizations

Reef Relief is an organization dedicated to educating the public about the importance of coral reefs and advocating for their protection.

You can offer to join the group or sign up for volunteer opportunities at their website. (www.reefrelief.org)

The Ocean Conservancy is an advocacy group that focuses on protecting the health of the oceans. Sign up for one of their "International Coastal Cleanups" to help remove debris from ocean shores. (www.oceanconservancy.org/)

## Careers

**Marine conservationist:** Marine conservationists work hands-on to protect, restore, and preserve ocean ecosystems. They may work for governments, environmental groups, zoos and aquariums, or other conservation organizations. They look to balance the long-term health of the ocean with human needs.

**Sustainable fishery management:** If you're interested in limiting the environmental damage of commercial fishing, you may be interested in a career in fishery management. Fishery managers come up with ideas for safer, more sustainable fishing methods and work to put them into practice with other members of the industry.

# FIND OUT MORE

## BOOKS

McCalman, Iain. ***The Reef: A Passionate History: The Great Barrier Reef from Captain Hook to Climate Change.*** New York: Scientific American/Farrar, Straus and Giroux, 2014.

Skomal, Greg. ***The Shark Handbook: Second Edition: The Essential Guide for Understanding the Sharks of the World.*** Kennebunkport, ME: Cider Mill Press, 2016.

Young, Karen Romano. ***National Geographic Kids Mission: Sea Turtle Rescue***. Washington, DC: National Geographic Children's Books, 2015.

## WEB SITES

Campbell, Andy. "Ocean Fish Populations Cut in Half Since the 1970s: Report." The Huffington Post, September 16, 2015. http://www.huffingtonpost.com/entry/crucial-marine-populations-cut-in-half-since-the-1970s-report_us_55f9ecd2e4b00310edf5b1b2.

Simpson, Sarah. "10 Solutions to Save the Ocean." Conservation Magazine, July 29, 2008. http://conservationmagazine.org/2008/07/10-solutions-to-save-the-ocean/.

# SERIES GLOSSARY OF KEY TERMS

**acidification** the process of making something have a higher acid concentration, a process happening now to world oceans

**activist** someone who works for a particular cause or issue

**biodiverse** having a large variety of plants and animals in a particular area

**ecosystem** the places where many species live, and how they interact with each other and their environment

**habitat** the type of area a particular type of animal typically lives in, with a common landscape, climate, and food sources

**keystone** a part of a system that everything else depends on

**poaching** illegally killing protected or privately-owned animals

**pollination** the process of fertilizing plants, often accomplished by transferring pollen from plant to plant

**sustain** to keep up something over a long period of time

**toxin** a poison

# INDEX



# PHOTO CREDITS

Adobe Images: Davidcarbo 22, Aleks White 25, Shuva Rahim 26, Fox 17, 39, Arnaudg22 40, andriisonlonchak 47, Wolgin 48, Wrangel 50, Stefanos Kyriazis 53, Piotyr Wawrzyniuk 58, Frantisek Hojdysz 60. Dreamstime.com: Whitcomberg 8, Peternile 10, Richard Carey 13, Bert Folsom 14t, Lehakok 17, Iakov Kalinin 18, MarleenWolters 20, Maxim Blinkov 29, Jonmilnes 43, Irina Igumnova 55, Sebastian Czapnik 56. Courtesy and with thanks to Maria Fuentes: 32. NOAA: 36, 44 (Richard Vevers KL Catlin Seaview Survey), Aiden Li 61. SHutterstock: Bildagentur Zoonar GmbH 30. Wikimedia: Scarlet23 16. US Fish and Wildlife Service/Ryan Hagerty: 6.

# ABOUT THE AUTHOR

**Michael Centore** is a writer and editor. He has helped produce many titles, including memoirs, cookbooks, and educational materials, for a variety of publishers. He has authored numerous books for Mason Crest, including titles in the Major Nations in a Global World and Drug Addiction and Recovery series. His work has appeared in the Los Angeles Review of Books, Killing the Buddha, Mockingbird, and other print- and web-based publications. He lives in Connecticut.